PENGUIN BOOKS

Glimmers

Cailin Hargreaves

Cailin Hargreaves is a writer and poet of North African descent living in London. At the age of 10 she developed an autoimmune disorder which attacks the lining of the colon, causing chronic pain and ulcers. She went from gymnastic lessons, piano practice to doctor's appointments and hospital rooms. She was old enough to understand what was happening but young enough to adapt well to her new reality.

Despite the turbulence and instability that came with navigating an autoimmune disease, she made it through the halls of university; graduating with a 2:1 in Politics and International Relations.

The trauma of facing mortality and accepting body's limitations at such a young age followed her into adulthood. She developed anxiety, which started as a small flickering candle but slowly erupted into a forest fire. Her words became her safe place, as she wrote to lay down her anger, heartache and fears without any feelings of judgment or shame. Unravel the chaos in her mind.

She started sharing beautiful writings on Instagram, and over the years, her account has grown into a platform that helps uplift and empower people throw the trials of life. She is currently boasts of 100k followers, and constantly growing. This journal is a beautiful means for readers to find help in coping with their trials, strengthening empathy and resilience.

Glimmers

YOUR DAILY JOURNAL FOR POSITIVE REFLECTION

Cailin Hargreaves

PENGUIN BOOKS

An imprint of Penguin Random House

PENGUIN BOOKS

Penguin Books is an imprint of the Penguin Random House group of
companies whose addresses can be found at
global.penguinrandomhouse.com

Published by Penguin Random House India Pvt. Ltd
4th Floor, Capital Tower 1, MG Road,
Gurugram 122 002, Haryana, India

Penguin
Random House
India

First published in Penguin Books by Penguin Random House India 2024

10 9 8 7 6 5 4 3 2

ISBN 9780143472780

Typeset in Adobe Garamond Pro by Digiultrabooks Pvt. Ltd.
Printed at Thomson Press India Ltd, New Delhi

www.penguin.co.in

MIX
Paper | Supporting
responsible forestry
FSC® C010615

Introduction

In these pages, I share with you the words that have illuminated my path. Life is full of hardships and dark moments that can leave scars. Yet, in those moments, we often find 'glimmers'-small yet shining moments of hope and happiness that lift us up, sparking gratitude and joy and providing shelter from the storms we frequently navigate.

Just as triggers can plunge us into the depths of painful traumas and memories, glimmers do the opposite. They remind us of the beauty and wonder that persist in the world, grounding us in the present and offering our hearts comfort and solace.

Each poem and illustration within this journal has been lovingly crafted, a personal gift from my heart to yours. They capture the depths of my experiences -the darkness, light, pain, and healing that life has given me. My hope is that in sharing these words, they will guide you on your unique journey of self-discovery and healing.

When the weight of the world feels overwhelming, I invite you to turn to these pages. Delve into the depths of your inner world, discover the treasures within, and harness the power of journaling to navigate life's ups and downs. Let the words, prompts, and images serve as your compass, directing you to the small, beautiful moments that exist both around and within you.

Consider this journal a sanctuary for reflection, visualisation, dreaming, and growth. Allow the glimmers of life to illuminate your path towards selflove, gratitude, hope, and joy. Remember, you are not alone. Just as recognising and acknowledging the glimmers in my life has supported me, I hope they will do the same for you, bathing you in their gentle light.

With all my heart,

Cailin

Journal Tips

Here are some tips on how to use this journal:

1) Be Consistent: Aim for regular entries, whether that's daily, every other day, or weekly. Consistency fosters a writing habit and deepens your connection with the journaling process.

2) Make it Personal: This journal is your sacred space. Let it reflect your thoughts, feelings, and experiences. There's no right or wrong way to journal; it's all about what feels best for you.

3) Stay Honest: Be truthful with yourself. Your journal is a safe space to express your raw, unfiltered thoughts and feelings without judgment.

4) Embrace All Emotions: Don't shy away from writing about negative feelings or experiences. Your journal can be a therapeutic space for you to explore these emotions and start healing.

5) No Pressure: Don't stress about grammar, punctuation, or spelling. This is your personal space and the only goal is self-expression and reflection.

6) Experiment with Formats: Feel free to mix up your writing style. You can write lists, letters, poems, or even draw sketches.

7) Use Prompts: If you're finding it difficult to start writing, use the prompts provided in this journal. They're designed to ignite your thoughts and encourage introspection.

8) Practice Gratitude: Try to regularly note down things you're grateful for. This simple practice can have a significant impact on your mindset and overall wellbeing.

9) Date your Entries: Keeping track of the date helps you to see your progress over time and reflect back on past thoughts and feelings.

10) Make it a Ritual: Create a calm and inviting space for your journaling time. Light a candle, play some soft music, and make it a special time for you.

Remember, the purpose of journaling is to learn more about yourself, foster self-growth, and navigate life more consciously. Enjoy the journey!

Joy

Introduction

Joy comes to us in ordinary moments. We risk missing out when we get too busy chasing down the extraordinary.

— Brené Brown

Life can at times feel like just an overwhelming number of tasks, responsibilities, and challenges that we need to get through, to accomplish something.

However, buried amongst the chaos, is this incredible thing called 'joy'. It's the genuine smile you can't help but share, the laughter that rises from deep within, the small joys of daily life or the wonderful, unexpected moments that take your breath away.

This chapter is dedicated to rediscovering and embracing those hidden and loud moments.

Think of this as your personal guide, filled with question to encourage reflection, poems to uplift, and illustrations to transport you into the world of your inner joy.

I'm here to remind you of all the times when joy snuck up on you in surpnsing new ways.

Consider the memory of a joke shared with a friend or family member that caused you to break out in uncontrollable laughter until tears raced down your face.

Maybe it's the feeling of success after achieving a relentlessly pursed goal, or the scent of rain kissing the Earth on a warm summer day that evokes a deep sense of contentment within you.

Everyone has personal memories, rituals, or hobbies that spark joy within them. This chapter is your sanctuary, a place to rekindle, cherish, and revel in these precious moments.

Joy isn't just an emotion; it's also deeply linked to the love and kindness we experience and share with others.

Dear reader, as you navigate this journey, my hope for you is that you rediscover a profound sense of gratitude for the beauty and joy that life offers us in every moment. Dive in, and let's celebrate the joy in our lives.

Remember the times when you couldn't stop smiling because you felt so joyful? Let's pause and go back to those special moments?

There are times you feel joyful just because you made someone else happy, let's share the story of how happiness can come from being the source of it.

happiness is a beautiful scent to wear
for when you walk past others
it lingers in the air

- cay

Let's talk about your daily doses of happiness! Let's list five things that never fail to bring a smile to your face?

Joy can come from personal achievements too! Let's remember every moment you accomplished something big or small, and couldn't help but beam with happiness?

Have you ever found joy in a challenging situation, a silver lining that kept you going? Let's recall that, and how holding onto silver linings are a joy too.

Is there a person in your life that always manages to make you happy? Tell me about them and why they light up your day?

Do you have a cherished piece of advice or wisdom that always lifts your spirits? Let's pause to share and think why it is special to you.

the little joys in life
often hide from view
but in the present moment
they reveal themselves to you

- there is beauty in the ordinary

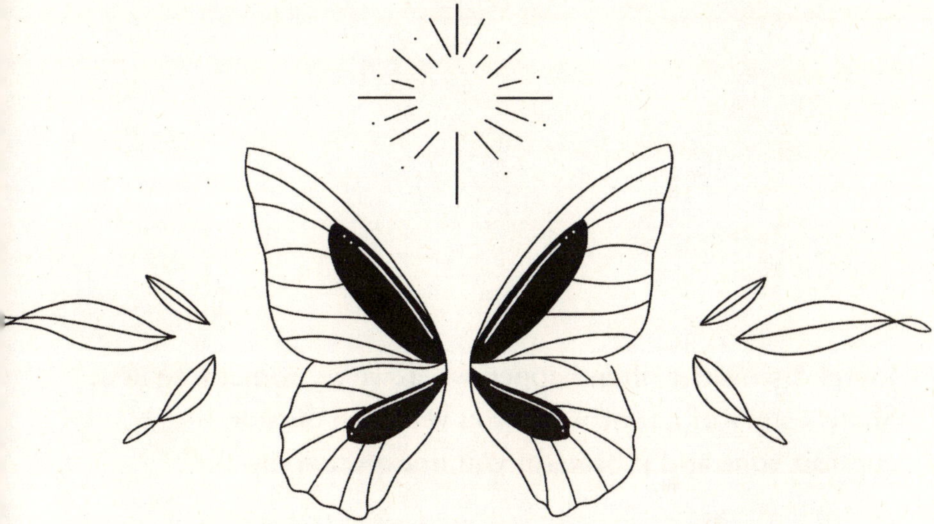

embrace joy daily

Do you have a cherished piece of advice or wisdom that always lifts your spirit and brings joy to your heart when you remember it? Let's pause to share and think why it is special to you.

Joyful discoveries often happen when we try something new. Share a story of a time when you ventured outside your comfort zone and it brought you unexpected joy.

Joyful moments often involve laughter. Can you recall a time when you laughed so hard that your stomach hurt? What was so funny, and why did it bring you such joy?

Let's take a walk down memory lane! Can you think of a childhood memory that still brings a big smile to your face? Why is it a joyous one?

when you start
doing things from your heart
life will show you how
every moment can be art

- fall in love with the beauty of today

Can you remember a moment when you were suprised by joy, perhaps through a kind gesture or piece of good news. What feeling did it leave you with?

If you were to write a note to your future self about a happy moment that you had today, what would it say?

Have you ever experienced a burst of happiness from witnessing a beautiful natural phenomenon, like a stunning sunrise or a beautiful rainbow. Let's paint a picture of this moment with words.

joy is the sunlight
that breaks through
the clouds

Imagine joy as a colour. Use paints or coloured pencils to create a pallette of this 'joy' with different shades and tones.

How do you feel as you look at these joyous hues?

What is your go-to happy song? Let's make a joy playlist below ...

Create a vibrant cover art for your joy playlist using any medium you prefer.

Let's write about what each song makes you feel every time you hear it

Picture a garden that grows all things joyful. Sketch or paint this garden and populate it with plants, creatures, and objects that represent joy to you.

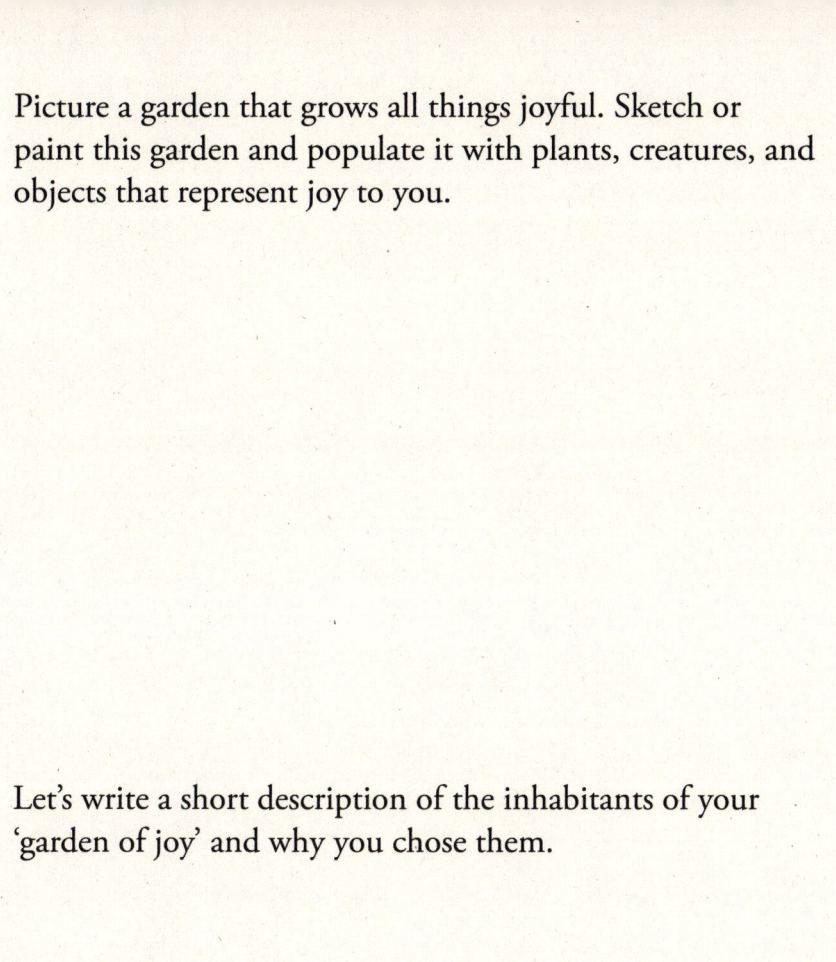

Let's write a short description of the inhabitants of your 'garden of joy' and why you chose them.

Reflection

As we reflect upon healing, let's take a moment to honor the transformative power it brings to our souls. Write down three affirmations that resonate with you. These affirmations could be words of encouragement, insights into your relationship with healing, or celebrations of moments when healing was your beacon of hope.

Example to inspire - Through healing, I rediscover my inner strength and serenity.

Before we proceed, let's embrace a moment of reflection. Pen a short note to yourself, expressing gratitude for the healing you've experienced and nurtured throughout this chapter. It could be a heartfelt acknowledgment of a time you overcame pain, or simply for recognizing the power of healing in your life.

Example to inspire - Thank you for honoring the journey and the strength that comes from embracing healing.

Patience

Introduction

Patience is not simply the ability to wait - it's how we behave while we're waiting.'

— Joyce Meyer

In today's fast-paced world where constant productivity and instant gratification are celebrated, the art of patience is often overshadowed. We've been programmed to expect immediate responses, quick solutions, and instant results. But in the middle of this persistent rush, there lies a captivating strength in patience. It's a gentle reminder of the beauty in waiting, the wisdom that arises from taking our time, and the power in letting life unfold naturally.

This chapter is an invitation to pause, reflect, and embrace the role of patience in your life. Through thoughtful questions, empowering verses and moments of quite contemplation, we'll explore all the times when patience gently revealed your inner grace. Perhaps it restored a strained relationship, shed light on a path to clarity, or unveiled unanticipated joys.

Keep in mind, patience isn't just a matter of watching the days pass you by, it's rather about how we journey through those days.

It's a conscious choice to believe that great things are birthed from our ability to put in the time and the effort needed to achieve them. It's the understanding that waiting can be an act of kindness, bravery, and love. Together, we'll dive into this concept, ensuring to appreciate how patience can be both a challenge and a reward in our lives.

Dear reader, as you immerse yourself in these words, do so with a free and open heart. Be honest with yourself by acknowledging the times when patience was your guiding star and the moments when you wish you had been able to summon it soon. Understand that you are still learning, and that every step you make, every pause you embrace, enriches your experience. Welcome to your journey through the depths of patience.

Can you think of a time when playing the patience game paid off in the end? How did you feel when you finally saw the positive outcome?

Let's recall a situation that truly tested your patience beyond your capacity, let's reflect on how and from where you drew the strength to endure and carry on?

Do you know someone who has the patience of a saint? How do you think they do it, what would you like to borrow from their approach?

Let's talk about the magic of patience. Do you think it enforces an introspection; you wouldn't have if you weren't made to wait?

How do you think patience helps in keeping your physical and mental health in check?

In what ways has giving patience a shot helped in smoothing things over in your relationships with your partner, friends and family?

When the pressure in on, what are your go-to moves to stay patient?

through love's alchemy
wounds transform into gold
so lay down all your weapons
and let tenderness take hold

- be patient with yourself

take as much time
as you need

Picture a version of yourself infused with boundless patience. How are you different from the person in this image? What would this person do differently or more of?

Explore a memory where you felt time was crawling by, yet looking back, you're grateful for that slow pace. Let's reflect on what that prolonged moment taught you?

Let's imagine nature: trees growing, flowers blooming, and rivers flowing. How does nature exemplify patience for you, and what inspiration can you draw from it?

two steps forward
one step back
depending on the day
but i know i will bloom
like the flowers do in may

-cay

In a world that's constantly rushing, how does patience serve as a grounding anchor for you? What imagery comes to mind?

Remember a time when someone showed you unexpected patience. How did their patience affect the way you saw them and the situation?

Imagine giving a gift of patience to someone. What would it look like, and how would it change their life?

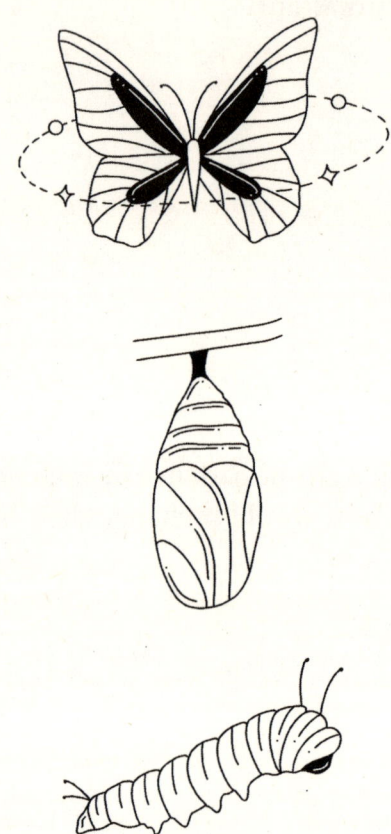

be strong enough
to wait for what
you deserve

If patience could gift you something, what would it be? Is it a physical object, a feeling, a memory, or a moment in time? Design and draw this gift below.

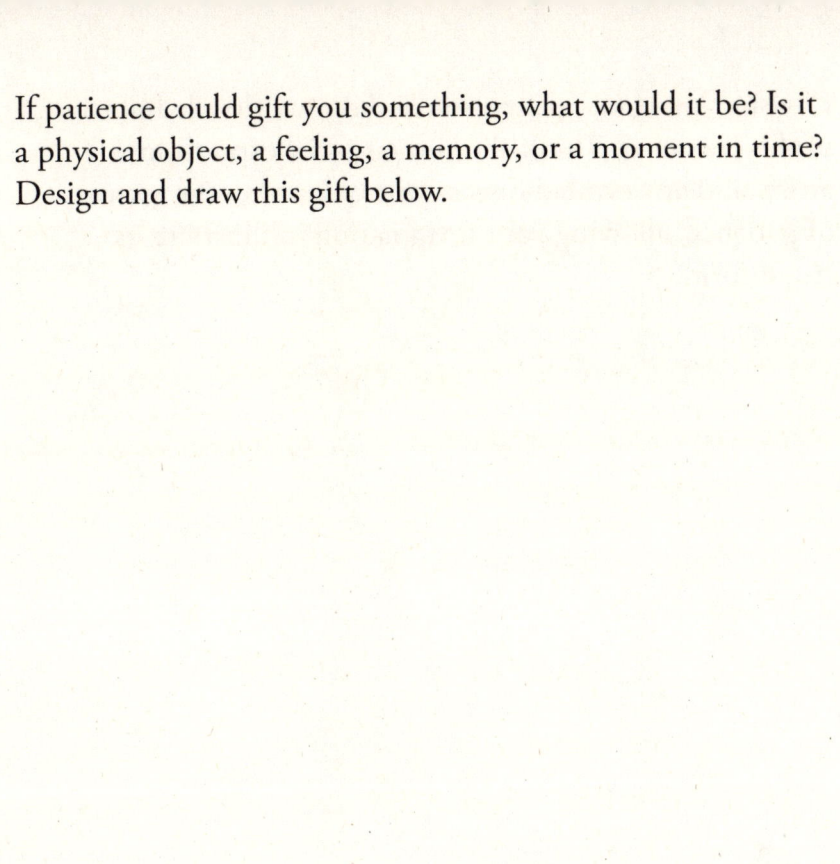

Write a thank-you note to patience for bestowing this gift upon you.

Envision 'patience' as a person and draw a detailed portrait of this character. Think about their facial expressions, attire, and any symbolic accessories. Capture, the essence of patience, allowing your imagination to illustrate its truest form.

Pen a letter to 'patience,' as though you're reaching out to a long time friend. Reflect on the moments you've leaned on their presence, express your appreciation, and contemplate the profound connection your share, recalling the challenges and triumphs you've faced together.

Example - Dear patience, I remember those quiet nights when you sat beside me, reminding me to breathe during moment of uncertainty.

Reflection

As we reflect upon healing, let's take a moment to honor the transformative power it brings to our souls. Write down three affirmations that resonate with you. These affirmations could be words of encouragement, insights into your relationship with healing, or celebrations of moments when healing was your beacon of hope.

Example to inspire - Through healing, I rediscover my inner strength and serenity.

Before we proceed, let's embrace a moment of reflection. Pen a short note to yourself, expressing gratitude for the healing you've experienced and nurtured throughout this chapter. It could be a heartfelt acknowledgment of a time you overcame pain, or simply for recognizing the power of healing in your life.

Example to inspire- Thank you for honoring the journey and the strength that comes from embracing healing.

Healing

Introduction

Healing is an art. It takes time, it takes patience. It takes love.

— Mazda Dohta

Life has a way of offering both beautiful and challenging moments, some of which may leave us with wounds; visible to all or hidden deep within the corners of our hearts. Our scars are a testament to our human experience and a reminder that we are not alone in our pain. Healing is not merely the act of eliminating our pain, but is an inward journey of rediscovery, a gentle process of self-acceptance amid the chaos life throws at us.

Please see these pages as a safe space to lay down all your pain without any fear of judgment. An environment that aims to honour and understand the wounds you have been carrying with you. With the use of gentle questions, comforting poems, and creative illustrations, we will explore your personal stories of recovery and awakening, making sure to celebrate the importance of every step along the way.

As you know, healing isn't linear; it's a path with ups and downs, with moments of clarity accompanied with moment of confusion.

Each step offers us lessons about the importance of forgiveness and gentleness, not just towards others but also towards ourselves. If this sounds a little daunting, don't worry, for I will be here alongside you to help navigate these moment together, recognising the hurdles whilst also pausing to honour every small win.

Dear reader, we will walk through the difficult days, the breakthroughs, the moments of renewed self-love, and acceptance. It's an invitation to take back your power, and though healing ebbs and flows, each step you take is a testament to the incredible strength and resilience that lives inside of you. As you engage with these prompts and reflections, I ask you to do so with a great deal of love and kindness towards yourself.

As we begin, take a moment to reflect on where you are now in your healing journey. What feelings or thoughts arise when you consider the progress you've made?

Can you pinpoint a part of your life that's blossomed positively through your healing journey? Let's dive into that.

be the safe place
that your heart needs to heal
the fragments of yourself
you have abandoned

- give yourself the love you need

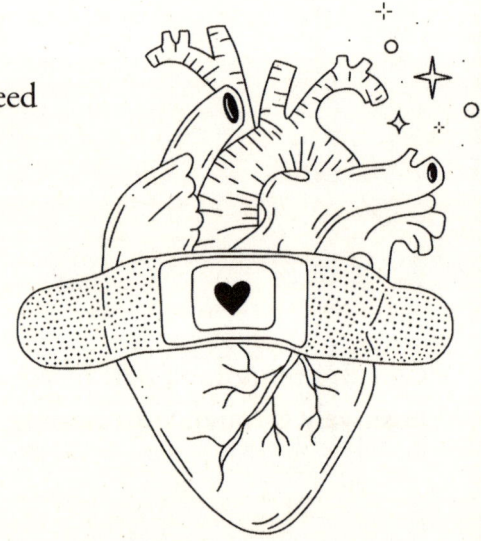

Through healing, we often learn to love ourselves a bit more. Can you list down five aspects of yourself that you've grown to appreciate or accept?

If you were to guide someone just stepping onto their healing path, what golden piece of advice would you offer them?

Was there a 'wow' moment when you realised just how far you've come in your healing journey? Let's hear about it!

Thinking back, are there any old habits or behaviours you've waved goodbye to as you've healed? Let's list and tick them off for good

In the mist of your healing journey, have you found any activities or practises that seem to help you along the way? How do they lift your spirit or change your mood?

every moment comes and goes
time slips through our fingers
like a river flows
so in this fleeting dance of life
embrace the highs and lows
let your heart breathe freely
so that love has space to grow

-cay

Come
home to
yourself

We all have those little affirmations or sayings that become our mantra. Do you have one that's been your anchor during challenging times?

It's often said that the company we keep impacts our path. Have any relationships or friendships evolved or deepened as you've healed?

What are some of the obstacles or challenges you've encountered on your healing journey? How have you overcome them?

Sometimes our environment plays a big part in our healing. Have any specific places - like a quiet park, serene beach, or cosy spot in your home - contributed to your growth? What makes these spots special?

be kind to
your heart

Visualise your healing journey as a canvas. What colours, shapes, and textures come to mind that represent your experiences? Use these elements to paint or draw your journey in the space below.

Take a closer look at each element on your canvas. Can you elaborate on what they symbolise? Describe how these elements capture specific moments or emotions from your journey towards healing.

Picture your healing journey as a voyage on the sea. What's your vessel? A grand ship or a simple boat? Along the way, have you navigated through storms, calm patches, or made unexpected discoveries? Sketch out a map of this voyage, making key landmarks and moments on your sea of healing.

Reflection

As we reflect upon patience, let's take a moment to honour the steady calm it brings to our lives. Write down three affirmations that resonate with you concerning this virtue. These affirmations could be words of encouragement, insights into your relationship with patience, or celebrations of moments when patience was your guiding star.

Example to inspire - With patience, I find clarity and peace.

Before we proceed, let's embrace a moment of gratitude. Pen a short note to yourself, expressing gratitude for the patience you've shown and nurtured throughout this chapter. It could be a heartfelt acknowledgment for a moment you waited gracefully, or simply for recognising the power of patience in your life.

Example to inspire - Thank you for honouring the growth that comes from practising patience.

Gratitude

Introduction

Gratitude makes sense of our past, brings peace for today, and creates a vision for tomorrow.

— Melody Beattie

In life's colourful combination of experiences, gratitude subtly emerges, gently nudging our hearts, reminding us of its presence, and inspiring us to recognize and celebrate the good in our lives. In this chapter, I warmly encourage you to immerse yourself in the power of this profound emotion, so that you may find both comfort and acknowledgment in the simple act of genuine appreciation.

Through the use of thoughtful prompts, expressive verses, and moments of thankful reflection, we'll dive into the occasions, both big and small, that have made you pause and reflect on the gratitude within you. It could be an unexpected act of kindness, a lesson learned through hardships, or the undeniable beauty of a peaceful sunset - every instance of gratitude anchors us steady through the storms of life.

It's not merely just a matter of listing things that you're grateful for but understanding why they hold value for you to begin with.

By exploring these feelings, we can find clarity in the past, peace in our present, and optimism for our future. Gratitude allows us to notice the silver linings, appreciate the path ahead of us, and notice the many ways in which we are supported.

Dear reader, as you make your way through these pages, allow gratitude to wrap itself around your heart and be your guide. Allow it to help you find the good in both the successes and the challenges you have endured. This journey is about creating a mindset where thankfulness becomes habitual, almost like brushing your teeth in the morning. So that it can enrich your life and amplify all the blessings around you that can sometimes go unnoticed.

Let's remember a time when your heart was just overflowing with gratitude. What sparked that feeling?

Is there a change in your mood or perspective when you express gratitude? Let's focus on what these changes are?

when we appreciate the beauty
in the little things that dwell
mindfulness becomes a gift
that we give to ourselves

-cay

Gifts From The
Universe

What are the top five little joys or blessings that you're thankful for today that have brightened your mood or day?

Often, the things we see every day become almost invisible to us. Is there something routine in your life that, upon reflection, fills you with a deep sense of gratitude?

Celebrate your uniqueness! What's a talent or skill you possess that you truly cherish? How does it illuminate and enhance your life?

Looking back, can you identify a tough period in your life that you've grown to be thankful for? How has it shaped you?

Have you ever been caught off guard by something unexpected that you ended up being grateful for? Share that moment?

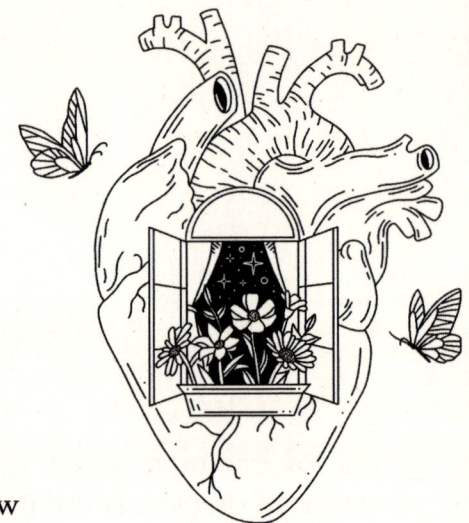

change is like a cracked window
flooding air into the dusty rooms
of our hearts

- embrace the birth of new beginnings

enjoy the little
things in life

Name an everyday object that adds comfort or convenience to your life. Why does it spark gratitude?

Which person in your life fills you with gratitude through their support or kindness? Is there a particular act of theirs that touched your heart recently?

What's a recent hobby or interest you've embraced that you're deeply thankful for? Maybe it's brought a renewed zest to your life.

Shared moments! Remember a recent gathering, event, or outing that left you feeling thankful. What was special about it?

with every sunrise
a symphony begins to play
unveiling all the possibilities
that are found in each new day

- leave the troubles of yesterday behind

Think of a mistake or setback you've experienced. In hindsight, what aspects of it are your thankful for, and how did it contribute to your growth?

there are tiny treasures
hidden in each moment

It's body appreciation time! What is something about your body or health that fills you with gratitude? Perhaps a feature or ability you especially cherish.

When you gaze outside, which natural wonders stir a sense of gratitude within you? Perhaps there's a particular sight or sound that especially resonates with your heart?

Imagine the night sky filled with illuminous stars of gratitude. Plot your own constellation, where each star represents a person or experience you're thankful for. Connect the stars and give your constellation a name. Describe the story or legend behind it.

If gratitude could be expressed through a playlist, what songs would you include? List the songs and write a brief description for each, explaining how it reflects your feelings of thankfulness and the emotions or memories it evokes.

Visualize a bookshelf, where every book symbolizes a cherished, gratitude-filled moment of your life. Select a few 'titles' and jot them down below.

Let's write down briefly what it is about and why it deserves a place on you shelf.

Reflection

As we reflect upon gratitude, let's take a moment to honor the joy and contentment it brings to our hearts. Write down three affirmations that resonate with you about this heartwarming sentiment. These affirmations could be words of appreciation, insights into your experiences with gratitude, or celebrations of moments when a simple "thank you" uplifted your spirit.

Example to inspire - With gratitude, I see the abundance in every moment and cherish life's gifts.

Before we proceed further, let's embrace a moment dedicated to gratitude itself. Pen a short note to yourself, expressing thanks for the times you've embraced gratitude and the positive shifts it has brought to your life. It could be a heartfelt acknowledgment of a moment you felt deeply thankful, or simply for recognizing the transformative power of gratitude.

Example to inspire - Thank you for recognizing and celebrating the many blessings, large and small, that make life richer and more meaningful.

Self Love

Introduction

To love oneself is the beginning of a lifelong romance.
— Oscar Wilde

More often than not, we end up being our own worst critics; by constantly striving for perfection and comparing ourselves to others. Developing self-love is similar to finding a treasure that has always been present within you, hidden under the layers of self-doubt and high expectations. Selflove is not the same as vanity; it's acknowledging and accepting that we deserve the same kindness, compassion and understanding we extend to those around us.

As you step into these pages, may the warmth extended through every word, poem, and image serve as a gentle whisper, reminding you of your worth and guiding you to recognise and celebrate the intrinsic value that resides within you. I invite you to become an active participant, reflecting on your journey to create a strong foundation of selflove, fused together by a sense of deep appreciation, acceptance, and acknowledgment for the extraordinary person that is you.

Each prompt will gently guide you, shining a light on your proudest accomplishments and revisiting challenging times to remind you of your capability to achieve great things.

It celebrates how much you've grown and transformed into the person you are at this very moment. Consider this chapter your personal retreat: a peaceful space where you're encouraged to have a heart-to-heart with yourself, lavishing it with the love and tenderness it deserves.

Dear reader, this path toward building a kinder, gentler, and more understanding relationship with yourself will teach you to be loving and patient, not only during good times but also in tough moments. Welcome to your personal adventure of self-love, where every word, message, and affirmation reminds you that you have always been enough.

Let's reflect on the ways you stand out from the crowd? Let's recognise your individuality and your unique journey.

How can you apply your own love language to yourself? Describe ways in which you can express self-love using your primary love language.

to reject parts of who you are
is to deny the beauty of the stars that formed you

- the universe does not make mistakes

Can you recall a time where a little more self-love and acceptance would have gone a long way? Would you like to approach similar situations lovingly in the future?

Time to brag! Can you list the milestones you've achieved that make you puff up with pride. No achievement is too small - each one is a testament to your journey and growth.

Your body does so much for you everyday! How about penning down a sweet note thanking it for all the wonders it allows you to do?

Remember a time when you firmly stood your ground? How did championing for yourself make you feel?

If you could send a heartfelt message to a younger you, what loving words of encouragement and wisdom would you share?

inside you are pieces
of the planets and the Earth,
you have always been divine,
since the moment you were birthed

- never forget your power

give yourself the
love you need

Think of a current challenge. How can you approach it with love, patience, and understanding towards yourself?

How can you sprinkle a little extra kindness on yourself today? Describe a small, loving gesture that you'll commit to doing; for yourself!

Close your eyes and visualise enveloping yourself in a warm, loving light. What emotions arise, and how can you hold onto them in your daily life?

your hearts innate desire to know love
is too great a burden
to settle for half given gestures
and empty promises
from those who want nothing
but to waste your time

-cay

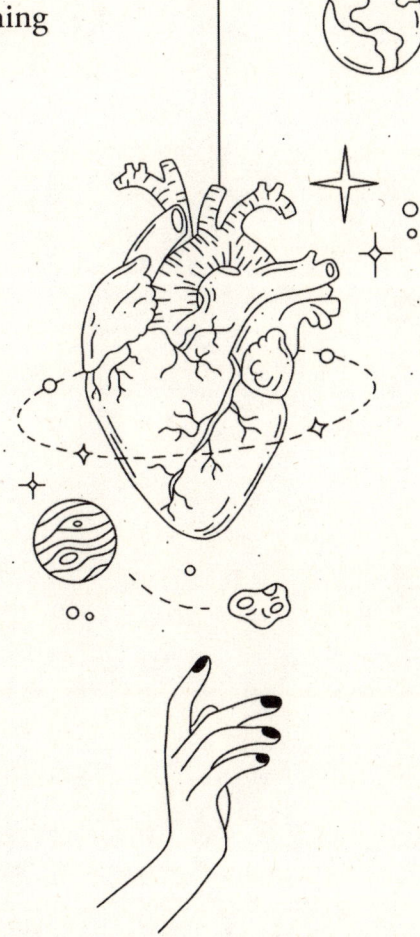

Let's brainstorm! Can you think of at least 5 little acts of love and care you can shower upon yourself daily?

Dream a little dream where you love yourself without any barriers. What magical transformations do you see in your life?

Spend a few moments gazing at your reflection with kindness. What are some loving affirmations you can tell your mirrored self today?

your soul is a
garden of love

Draw ajar below and fill it with short notes of compliments and praise for yourself, highlighting your qualities that you would never want to lose. Consider colouring each note differently, representing various aspects ofyourself ... take as much room as you'd like.

Create a 'recipe' for self-love. List 'ingredients' like personal strengths, happy memories, and valued achievements. Next, write detailed directions on how to combine and use these ingredients in your daily life for a stronger sense of self-worth. Finish by decorating your recipe with colours that make you happy!

Visualise a mirror that reflects not only your physical self but your inner self. Around this mirror, write down all the kind words and phrases that you would like the mirror to tell you daily.

Reflection

As we reflect upon self-love, let's take a moment to honor the gentle embrace it offers to our being. Write down three affirmations that resonate with you about this profound relationship with oneself. These affirmations could be words of encouragement, insights into your journey of self-love, or celebrations of moments when loving yourself was a transformative experience.

Example to inspire - Through self-love, I am my own anchor, my own cheerleader.

Before we continue, let's capture a moment of gratitude. Pen a short note to yourself, expressing appreciation for the self-love you've cultivated and cherished in this phase of your life. It could be a heartfelt acknowledgment of a time you chose yourself over external pressures, or simply for recognizing the importance of self-worth.

Example to inspire - Thank you for honoring the love I have for myself, and understanding its foundational role in my life.

Courage

Introduction

Courage is not the absence of fear, but the triumph over it.
— Nelson Mandela

Picture your life as a vibrant, unfolding narrative where every new chapter tells its own tale of courage-those moments when you faced challenges yet stood firm, the silent battles you waged, and the internal storms you've weathered. Each tale shines a light on times when courage served as your guiding force, enabling you to confront fears and rise above tough moments. Courage doesn't erase fear; it acknowledges it, accepts its presence, and resolves to forge ahead, fuelled by a flame of boldness and hope that burns brightly within our hearts.

Immerse yourself in this chapter, allowing it to gently open your heart and guide you through the pivotal moments where courage took centre stage in your life. With a spirit of tenderness, introspection, and appreciation, this section will unfurl into a haven for you to revisit, honour, and illuminate your moments of bravery and the lessons learned that have kindled flames of courage within you.

Leap into each reflection, retracing your steps through times of hardship where you confronted your own darkness and stood resiliently. Allow this space to serve as a sanctuary where fear loses its power over you. Trace your victories and extend appreciation to those who have exemplified courage in your life or taught you how to wear bravery boldly. As you complete each page, encourage yourself to jot down your stories of strength and determination with pride, so that you cease to downplay your resilience and instead celebrate it fiercely, for it has expertly guided you through the toughest moments of your life.

Dear reader, as you embark on this journey, may you uncover a renewed sense of strength, recognising and honouring the bold spirit within you. Welcome to your odyssey of courage.

Let's go back to a moment when fear unexpectedly taught you a lesson about courage? How did that experience change you?

Recall a time when you had to gather your courage to say something difficult. How did it go and what did you learn?

do not be afraid
to take a shot in the dark
for the dreams not pursued
will eat at the heart

-cay

Who is your courage superstar, someone who just embodies bravery so beautifully? What lessons can you soak up from them?

What do you think makes up courage? Share the elements that build bravery for you and how you see them in your actions.

Picture a 'you' one year from now, brimming with courage. What little habits do you see yourself overcoming, that come in the way of your resilience and bravery?

Share a time when you were touched by someone else's act of bravery. How did it positively affect you?

Is there a place where you feel exceptionally brave? Describe what makes it so speacial and why it gives you courage.

life will always bring you
to the place where you belong
so make peace with the journey
and remember to be strong

-cay

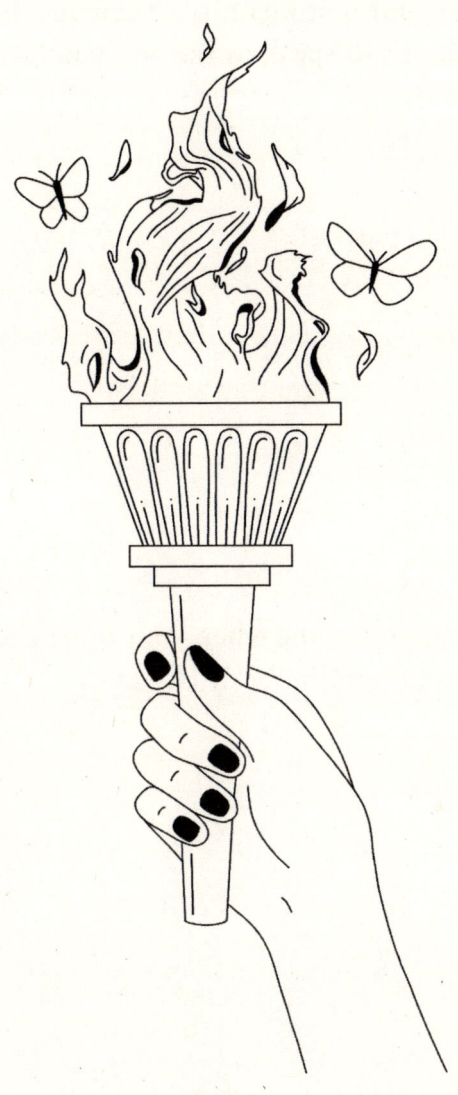

let the fire in you
burn relentlessly

Let's go back to your first memory of courage. How does that moment still speak to the way you face challenges today?

Can you share about a time when your quiet courage made all the difference, even if nobody else saw it?

Think back to a time when you were brave but things didn't go as planned. What did this setback teach you about courage?

Apologising can be a courageous act, can't it? Share a time when you mustered up the bravery to apologise and how it transformed the situation.

darling
have no fear
with the endings
new beginnings will appear

-cay

Ever been suprised by your own bravery? Write about a time when you acted more courageously than you thought you were capable of.

Bravery can sometimes come with a cost, can't it? Share a time when being courageous came with a sacrifice or loss. How did you navigate through it?

Think of a personal 'mountain' you've conquered with your courage. What was the journey to the summit like, and what did the view from the top teach you?

fear is the shadow
courage is the sun

Imagine yourself as a hero of a tale where you overcome a great obstacle. Sketch yourself in the heroic attire that represents your inner strength in the box below. Then write down the attributes and skills that helped you in overcoming the challenge.

Craft a gallery titles 'Moments of Courage.' Document your favourites instances big or small, where you displayed bravery. For every moment create an 'exhibit card' below and write a brief description with symbols, illustrations or colours that capture the feeling of courage. Continue onto the following page if needed.

Design a personal crest filled with symbols and colours that represent your unique journey of courage and resilience. Below it, write a motto that embodies your philosophy on bravery.

Reflection

As we reflect upon courage, let's take a moment to honor the strength and bravery it imparts to our spirit. Write down three affirmations that resonate with you about this valorous quality. These affirmations could be words of encouragement, insights into your experiences with courage, or celebrations of moments when facing fears became a milestone.

Example to inspire - With courage, I conquer challenges and rise stronger than before.

Before we continue, let's pause for a moment of gratitude. Pen a short note to yourself, expressing appreciation for the courage you've displayed in this chapter of your life. It could be a heartfelt acknowledgment of a time you stepped out of your comfort zone, or simply for recognizing the resilience that courage instills.

Example to inspire - Thank you for the brave heartbeats and the steps taken in the face of adversity, embodying true courage.

Detachment

Introduction

Detachment is not that you should own nothing, but that nothing should own you.

— Ali ibn Abi Talib

Navigating through life's varied paths, our souls can frequently become entangled and burdened by our attachments-to people, possessions, and past memories. Detachment emerges as a liberating perspective, encouraging us to immerse ourselves fully without becoming bound or defined by these very engagements. It introduces a way of fully experiencing the beauty and wonder of life without anchoring ourselves to its inherent highs and lows, reminding us that our intrinsic nature remains untouched by the external realities of this world.

As you step into this section, you'll discover a tranquil oasis gently nudging you to explore the realms of detachment. Through evocative prompts, touching poetry, and mindful illustrations, the goal is to highlight various aspects of detachment, focusing on its transformative power to enrich our experiences and anchor our hearts and minds.

As you engage with each prompt, you'll be gently guided to reevaluate your connections and identify the essence of true attachment. This section serves as an invitation to honour your commitments to the world while cultivating an inner sanctuary of peace and tranquillity. It's about discovering the freedom that arises when we are not possessed by our possessions or chained to external entities.

By practising detachment, you open the doors to a world where you can live more authentically, love more profoundly, and remain free in spirit and essence.

Dear reader, welcome to your voyage of detachment, a journey toward inner freedom and more meaningful interactions with the people in your life.

When you think about detachment, what emotions surface? Are they more comforting or perhaps a little uneasy?

Can you recall the first time you consciously chose to detach from something; for your wellbeing? Let's recall the feelings and outcomes that unfolded.

you are made from the same magic
that fills the universe
so don't waste your time
convincing people of your worth

-you are *effortlessly* beautiful

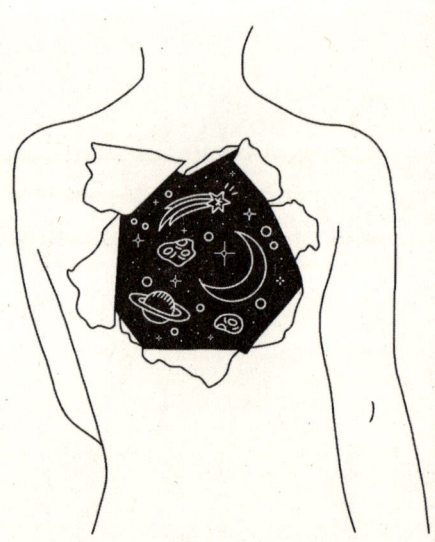

Reflect on the values that detachment can bring into your life. Share a personal story where detaching aligned with your inner values and brought clarity.

Explore an instance where detaching from a material possession brought unexpected emotions or realisations to the surface.

Have you ever found yourself detaching from a longheld belief or value? What was that like? Let's explore the journey and the transformation that came with it.

Do you think there is there a chapter in your life right now where sprinkling a little detachment could do wonders?

Explore a situation where detachment brought about regrets or second thoughts. Would you navigate it differently now?

Can you recall witnessing someone else practising detachment in a way that left an impression on you? What unfolded, and how did it impact your view on letting go.

i know forgiveness is hard
and healing can be slow
but as you learn to let go
peace begins to flow

- keep holding onto hope

serenity blooms in the
garden of release

Have you encountered any role models or teachings that encourage a healthy approach to detachment? Share your insights.

Let's visualise your life with a newfound sense of detachment; what changed do you foresee, and how would they benefit you?

Describe a moment when detachment felt like freedom. How did creating distance from a person, situation, or emotion impact your peace of mind?

like a river flows to sea
we must have the strength to walk
the paths that set us free

-trust your inner guidance

How do you balance attachment and detachment in your relationships? Can you think of a harmonious blend?

Have you ever detached from something only to reattach to it in a healthier way? Describe the process and emotional journey involved.

What is the most significant lesson detachment has taught you so far? Share a story that encapsulates this learning.

Share a moment when detachment from a role or identity created a shift in your self-perception and life narrative.

peace flows when
I gently let go

Craft a visual and descriptive river where each floating item represents something you're letting go of. Illustrate and write down why each item is on the river and the tranquillity or turbulence you feel as it floats away.

Create a 'time capsule' by listing down items or thoughts you wish to gently let go of. Explain why you chose each item and how detaching from it can benefit your future self.

Draw a wisdom tree below, with each branch representing a lesson or insight you have gained about letting go. Hang quotes, advice, or reflections directly from the branches, each sharing a unique piece of wisdom from your expereinces of detachment.

Reflection

As we reflect upon detachment, let's take a moment to honor the freedom and peace it grants to our minds. Write down three affirmations that resonate with you concerning this liberating principle. These affirmations could be words of encouragement, insights into your journey with detachment, or celebrations of moments when letting go transformed your perspective.

Example to inspire - Through detachment, I find clarity and embrace the ebb and flow of life.

Before we progress, let's hold a moment of gratitude. Pen a short note to yourself, expressing appreciation for the detachment you've practiced and integrated into this phase of your life. It could be a heartfelt acknowledgment of a time you released burdens not meant for you, or simply for recognizing the tranquility that detachment offers.

Example to inspire - Thank you for valuing inner peace and understanding the strength in graceful detachment.

Softness &
Vulnerability

Introduction

**Vulnerability is not winning or losing; it's having the courage to
show up and be seen when we have no control over the outcome.**
— Brene Brown

In the grand orchestra of our existence, vulnerability and softness
play soft yet strong tunes that echo the heartfelt truths of our shared
humanity. These qualities create connections from heart to heart,
allowing us to resonate with each other's joys, pains, and deepest
desires. Vulnerability, with its authenticity, and softness, with its gentle
embrace, encourage us to lower the walls around our hearts, and step
into a space of genuine connection and understanding.

In this section, you'll find a gentle embrace that honours the touching
beauty and bravery inherent in vulnerability and softness. Through
thoughtfully crafted prompts, emotionally resonant poetry, and tender
illustrations, you will embark on a journey to gently unravel the delicate
threads of these crucial states of being, illuminating their transformative
potential in our lives.

As you navigate each reflection, brace yourself to plunge into your own
depths, exploring reservoirs of memories and emotions.

This becomes your safe space to revisit moments of your own
vulnerability, to honour instances where softness has left a profound
imprint in your heart, and to recognize the strength within these
moments of pure authenticity.

Dear reader, as you walk through these pages, may you find comforting solace in the hands of vulnerability and softness, recognising them as steadfast companions in life's dance. Welcome to your exploration of vulnerability and softness, a sincere heart-to-heart with the raw and radiant aspects of your being.

Think back to a time when being vulnerable was your bravest act. What happened when you let those walls come down?

How do you think society views vulnerability and softness? Does it celebrate them or perhaps undervalue them?

though life can break us all
in many different ways
i hope that the softness
of your heart always stays

-cay

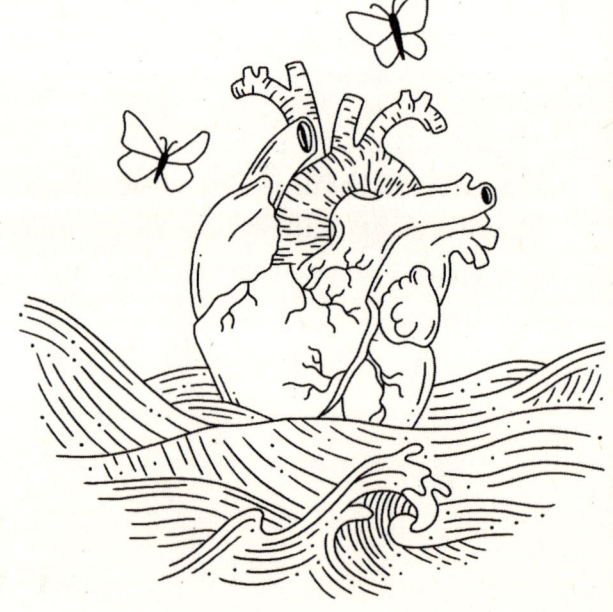

Reflect on how vulnerability plays a role in your friendships. How does being open and soft impact your connections?

Can you share a moment when you vulnerability or softness became a catalyst for personal growth and transformation?

Can you recall instances of softness that may go unnoticed or unacknowledged in your daily life? How do these moments of gentle presence feel?

If you were to advise someone on how to embrace vulnerability and softness, what would you say?

Explore a moment where softness became your strength. How did gently navigating through a situation lead to a positive outcome?

Recall an instance where you witnessed vulnability in someone else. How did that are you feel, and did it alter your perception of them?

leave your clothes at the door
not the ones that dress your skin
but the ones that cover your scars
unravel the layers you have wrapped
around your vulnerability
so i can feel the nakedness
of your soul

-cay

wear your softness
boldly

How do you practise softness towards yourself, especially during times when you might normally be critical or harsh?

Are there environments or scenarios where practising softness feels particularly challenging for you? Delve into exploring why this might be.

Do you think your cultural background and cultural perspectives have influenced your own views? Did you have to evolve beyond your cultural conditioning?

scars are proud monuments
of strength
laden with the battles
you have fought to still be here

- wear them with pride

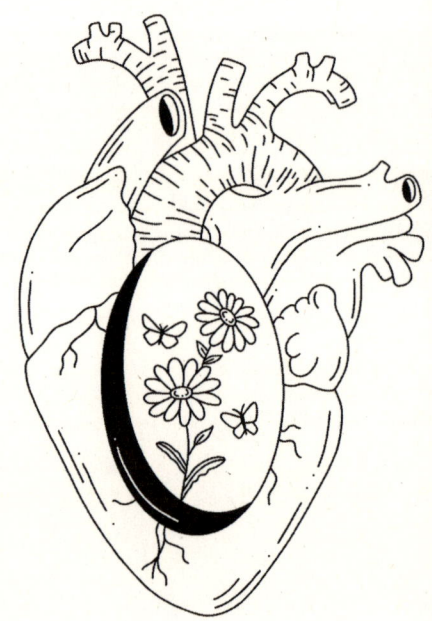

Dive into exploring how softness plays a role in your self-care routine. How does embracing gentleness towards yourself manifest in daily practices?

Share a time when you successfully balanced being soft yet firm. How did maintaining this equilibrium affect the outcome and your internal state?

Describe a moment where your softness or gentleness became a gift to someone. How did your soft demeanour impact the situation or person involved?

Are there specific barriers that make it challenging for you to embrace vulnerability? Let's talk about these obstacles and their origins.

honour the vulnerability
within you

If softness was a person, what kind of friend would they be? Write a letter to Softness, expressing your feelings, your fears, and your hopes in nurturing a friendship with it. What questions would you ask, and what would you hope to learn from your new friend?

Open your heart and create an art piece that represents what vulnerability and softness feel like to you. Use colours, shapes, and textures without focusing on creating recognisable objects. Afterwards, write down what arose during the creation and what you see and feel from the completed art.

Identify an area in your life where you resist vulnerability. Create an action plan using words and symbols on how to gradually introduce softness into this space without overwhelming yourself.

Reflection

As we reflect upon vulnerability and softness, let's take a moment to honor the authenticity and gentleness they bring into our lives. Write down three affirmations that resonate with you concerning these intertwined qualities. These affirmations could be words of solace, insights into your journey with both vulnerability and softness, or celebrations of moments when embracing these traits led to deeper connections and understanding.

Example to inspire- Through vulnerability and softness, I connect genuinely, fostering bonds built on trust and empathy.

Before we continue, let's pause for a moment of gratitude. Pen a short note to yourself, expressing appreciation for the times you've allowed vulnerability and softness to guide your actions and relationships. It could be a heartfelt acknowledgment of a time you laid bare your emotions, or simply for recognizing the strength that lies in gentleness and openness.

Example to inspire- Thank you for embracing the power of vulnerability and the grace of softness, understanding that they together are a testament to true strength.

Kindness & Compassion

Introduction

Whenever there is a human being, there is an opportunity for kindness.

— Seneca

In the hustle-bustle of everyday life and the challenges of our daily routines, kindness and compassion emerge as silent, yet powerful forces capable of reshaping not only our individual journeys but also the nature of society. They are the bridges that connect our individual experiences to each other, the gentle touches that help heal our emotional wounds, and offer unspoken recognition that make us feel loved and understood by the people around us.

In this section, you are invited to explore the profound impact of kindness and compassion in your life, and in the lives of those around you. With every thoughtful prompt, empathetic poem, and soothing illustration, you'll have a refuge to purposely reflect on these virtues and understand the profound influence they've had on your path.

Give yourself the freedom to engage deeply with each prompt, recalling moments where a compassionate gesture, or a simple act of kindness transformed an ordinary day into something memorable.

Give thanks to the people who have shown these qualities to you and consider the times when you were able to light up someone else's world with your own kindness and compassion.

This chapter is more than a collection of words; it's a testament to the endless potential hidden inside every act of kindness and compassion, illuminating the lives of those around you.

Dear reader, as you wander through these pages, may you be inspired not only to recognize and appreciate acts of kindness and compassion but also to intertwine them into the fabric of your own life. Welcome to your journey of kindness and compassion -an exploration into the heart of human connection and benevolence.

Let's talk about what kindness and compassion mean to you personally. How would you define these beautiful traits?

How do you express kindness and compassion towards yourself, especially during challenging times? Share a moment when self-kindness made a difference.

i passed a stranger on the street
who shared with me a smile
and it pierced through the darkness
i'd been walking with for miles

- the power of kindness

Little drops make an ocean right? How do small daily doses of kindness touch your life?

Describe an ocassion where kindness acted as a bridge, either mending, connecting, or enhancing a relationship or situation in your life.

Do you have any plans for a kind gesture or a few compassionate words for someone today? What are you thinking of doing or saying?

Have you been on the receiving end of a kind gesture or comforting words lately? How did that feel?

Explore ways in which you might cultivate spaces (physical, emotional, or virtual) that nurture and encourage kindness and compassion.

How has your expression and understanding of kindness evolved over the years? Are there pivotal moments that shaped your relationship with being kind?

life can be hard
and the world can feel unkind
so let your compassion
be a light that someone finds

-cay

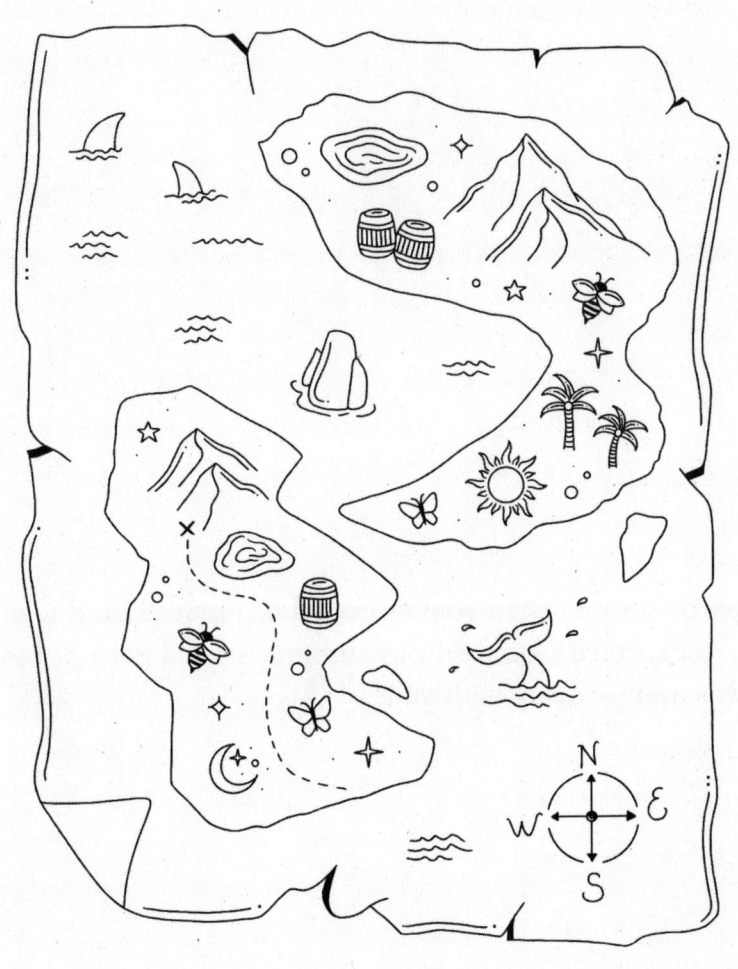

a gentle heart guides
my journey

Discuss a situation where extending compassion was difficult for you. What internal or external barriers were present and how did you navigate them?

Reflect on a time when you witnessed or received kindness in an unexpected place or from and unexpected person. How did this moment stay with you?

Reflect on a time when adopting a kind and compassionate communication style transformed a conversation or relationship.

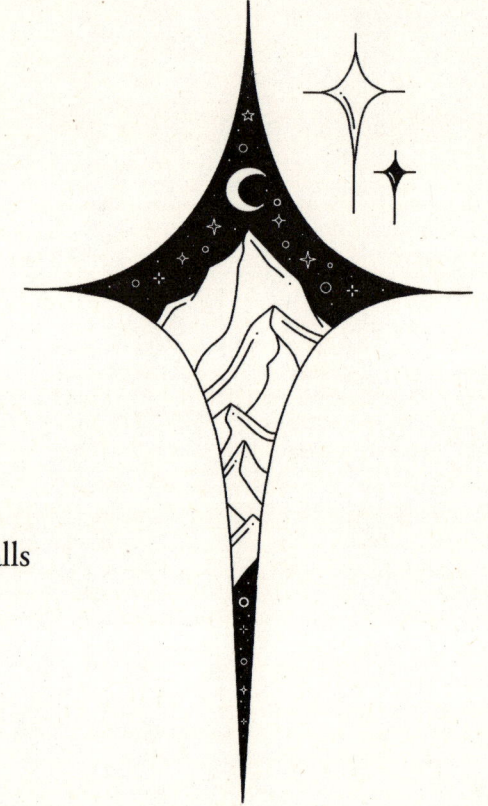

kindness is the sun
that carries every dawn
and even when the night falls
its warmth is never gone

-cay

Share an instance where showing compassion towards someone who wronged you brought about change, either in them, you, or the situation.

Explore your experience with compassion fatigue. How do you replenish yourself when your reservoirs of compassion feel depleted?

Examine your relationship between maintaining personal boundaries and being kind and compassionate. How do you balance the two?

Imagine waking up in a world overflowing with kindness and compassion. What changes you feel will take place around you?

let your actions
bloom from
kind intentions

Create a collage using images, words, or phrases from magazines and various sources that represent kindness and compassion to you. Select each item for your collage as a reflection of your own stories or wishes about becoming more kind and compassionate.

Take a moment to reflect and write about how to incorporate these collage elements into your daily practices, gently guiding your path towards a consistent and authentic embrace of kindness and compassion in you life.

Picture a gentle breeze that carries messages of kindness and compassion to you. Write down the messages you imagine it would whisper to you during tough times, giving you comfort and understanding.

Create a box filled with warmth and kindness, symbolized through your favorite compassionate scenes from movies or books. Describe these moments and reflect on how sharing this box would affect both you and the recipient's emotions.

Reflection

As we reflect upon kindness and compassion, let's take a moment to honor the warmth and understanding these virtues bring to our hearts. Write down three affirmations that resonate with you. These affirmations could be words of encouragement, insights into your relationship with kindness and compassion, or celebrations of moments when these values illuminated your path.

Example to inspire - With kindness and compassion, I bridge gaps and heal wounds.

Before we move forward, let's pause for a moment of gratitude. Pen a short note to yourself, expressing appreciation for the kindness and compassion you've extended and received in this chapter of your life. It could be a heartfelt acknowledgment of a time you comforted someone in need, or simply for recognizing the power of these virtues in shaping your interactions.

Example to inspire - Thank you for embracing the beauty that lies in acts of kindness and compassion.

Final Words

As we turn the final pages of "Glimmers," I hope you carry the light you've created in this journal into every corner of your world. The courage you've displayed throughout these pages, not only to face but also to embrace your inner world, is nothing short of inspiring. I want you to recognise and acknowledge the significance of this moment. In choosing to walk along this path, you've taken profound steps towards your own healing and self-discovery.

It has been an honour to share this experience with you, to provide glimmers of hope and joy that, I hope, have illuminated the darkest corners of your heart and mind. As we part ways, we know that this is not the end but rather the birth of a new beginning. Your journey doesn't stop when you close the journal. Instead, it's a chance to carry these glimmers with you into your daily lives and remind others of their presence as well.

In these pages, you've cultivated a garden of self-love, gratitude, and acceptance. Now the time has come to let these flowers bloom from these pages into the external world. It may seem daunting and nerve-wracking to take the next step, but I know you have built the strength and courage to carry the lessons, insights, and peace you've found within you into your everyday life. You should be overwhelmingly proud of the work you've done.

In choosing to face the darkness within, you've also chosen to step into the light and rest in the power of vulnerability, which is no easy feat. My wish for you is that you always remember how capable and courageous you are in navigating the challenges life throws your way.

As we say goodbye, I offer you these final words: continue to seek out the glimmers in every moment, those small sparks of joy, hope, and gratitude that light up the path towards a more joyful, richer, and fulfilling life. Trust that no matter how challenging the path ahead of you may get, you have made it through every difficult day of your life so far. No matter what happens, you will make it through any more that come your way.

With endless love and support,

Cailin.